Growth Hacking

By Jess Tiffany

Table of Contents

Acknowledgments

I would like to thank my wife for putting up with the craziness, that most of us entrepreneurs put our families through. We have faced some challenges over the years and she is steadfast in taking care of me and our four wonderful children. Our four kids are truly our joy and passion in life. We love them beyond measure! They are my giggle partners, exchanging jokes and silliness to rival any comedy crew in the world. They keep me motivated and feeling much younger than my age.

Thank you to my Mom, who has been a huge support in all my dreams, constantly telling me I could do it, even if she was not so sure. Dad, thank you for always trying to set me on a good course, I have always appreciated that. When you would stumble and fall, you always strive to get back up again.

Lastly, I would like to thank Christ Jesus, who profoundly changed my life, His inspiration, teaching and sacrifice has changed my life forever. Though I continually fail to walk in your example, and even though I am not worthy of your love, you never fail me.

MNU digital.

As more people take our online e-courses it became evident that many people needed additional help in the journey to success. This lead to the spin-off to the Marketing and Networking University called the M.N.U. Digital agency. M.N.U. Digital is a full service agency.

Services include:

- Web Design
- Search Engine Optimization
- Paid Advertising
- Graphic Design and Branding
- Email Marketing
- Social Media Management
- Marketing Strategy
- LinkedIn Overhaul Service

Marketing and Industry Domination with Jess Tiffany

As a business and marketing strategist, Jess is very passionate about our in-depth service offerings like finding businesses $50k in hidden revenue opportunities in under an hour. Upon request Jess coaches businesses to higher revenue, lead generation strategies, joint venture creation, unique proposition isolation and implementations and over 100 dynamic business strategies to cause mass growth in company sales and profits.

For those who are unable to work with Jess, he does offer an online version called the 52 Week Industry Domination Training. This program has been called "the most powerful and dynamic client attraction program ever created!" It also has been featured on Fox, NBC, CBS and ABC. This amazing program will take you through some of the most powerful business fundamentals that are overlooked and lead to most businesses failings. It continues on teaching proven advanced marketing skills and ultimately if implemented these skills will lead many businesses on to millions of dollars in revenue.

Learn more about Jess' 52 Week Industry Domination Training Today!

FIRST THINGS FIRST

Included in Who's Who in America and the World. Listed as top 250 Growth Hackers (Marketer) for 2018 via Goodman Lantern

Quality vs. Quantity?

Social Media has opened up opportunities for the masses to reach out to people from all walks of life. We are no longer limited to the neighborhood or city we live in to meet new people. Many of the younger generation have embraced this idea and will talk to anyone in the world more or less if they share a common interest. Gamers play online multi-player video games, people on iPhones and Android devices play chess and all sorts of games via apps with people from all over. Sometimes, you develop friendships or find true love through this medium.

We as business people have access to the same mediums, technologies and social media outlets. So why are so many people still opposed to or afraid of embracing the power of platforms like LinkedIn to grow their business and outreach?

When I talk about growing your LinkedIn connections, I get many people that are instantly offended by the idea. Many people say things like: Well, you can't get to know all those people, or I don't want to be connected to all those worthless connections.

First of all shame on you, those are people you are talking about. Everyone has value! (A few exceptions with fake profiles etc.) According to Omni Core Agency *https://www.omnicoreagency.com/linkedin-statistics/* over 44% of the users on LinkedIn make over $75,000 per year in income. So even if you guess terribly, you have a pretty good chance at connecting with someone of value. Additionally, 41% of Millionaires use LinkedIn. So there is a good chance a few of your connections may even be a Millionaire.

Secondly, who said connect to just any random person you can spam with an invite. Why not have quality and quantity. You don't have to give up one to have the other.

If I have not shook their hand then they can't be in my network, is not a good long term plan for growth. These same business owners five minutes later can be heard complaining about the price of online advertising. How they have to pay so much money to get a new customer or even a lead.

I have to recap here. I do not want someone to be in my network unless I have met them personally, so I pay tons of money to find people that have never heard of me, do not have a "connection" to me or my company, and have no thoughts of loyalty or reciprocity. **Did I mention you pay money for this lower quality, more risky, less mutually beneficial relationship?**

So, I would ask would you rather shop from an ad on Facebook from someone you have never met, - or, from a person you have not met before in person but have been passively reading about, gaining value from, learning from, getting inspired by their weekly quotes and developing a measure of trust from? I know this is a tough one!

The average customer must be exposed to you or your brand 7 to 30 times to feel comfortable to interact and make a purchase. So which is cheaper, your LinkedIn profile or Google Adwords?

What if you put a little strategy behind your network growth?

1.) Who are my ideal clients?

2.) Who are my dream clients?

3.) As my company grows what talent pool will I need access to?

4.) Think who would make a great joint venture partner?

5.) Good immediate mentors or collaborators?

6.) Dream mentors, favorite speakers or authors?

> **You never know what can happen when you reach out to new people.**

By building your network with purpose, you gain free advertisement opportunities, the chance to network with, learn about and build relationships with the type of people you would ideally serve. You still get to have your tight close friends from your inner circle. You still can grab a coffee with someone you met at a networking event. However, now you have the ability to build new quality relationships and possibly become friends with your dream clients or dream members.

Maybe 3 years from now you write a LinkedIn post about some new product your company developed and your dream client sees the post. He thinks it is lame, but an unknown even bigger fish sees it on your dream clients feed and reaches out to you to make a purchase. Just being associated with your dream clients on LinkedIn can possibly lead to a massive benefit, by association.

You never know what can happen when you reach out to new people. Have some conversations on the phone or with Skype, Zoom, etc. etc. I know from personal experience this works and brings amazing opportunities. I have met business leaders that charge thousands of dollars to have a meeting with them normally, and now I can call just to chat. I have met authors who have given me priceless advice on this project. Influencers with hundreds of thousands of connections that know who I am and would love to catch a coffee when or if we are ever close enough to make it happen. Wonderful people I met on LinkedIn and after a 15 minute chat on the phone want to contribute their thoughts for articles I am writing. Some even volunteer to write a blog post for my company. None of these and many more fantastic opportunities would have happened if I did not strategically build an amazing network. I believe the successes I have are not unique to me and can happen for you as well. It does not need to be on LinkedIn, I have also met incredible people on Twitter, BeBee, Alignable, Facebook, Xing and others. It just so happen that LinkedIn has been by far the best network for me to build my business and my brand.

INTRODUCTION

A lot of people have asked me how I went from having zero followers on LinkedIn to having 10,000 followers. It was a lot of work, but it was certainly worth the time and energy to build a great network of diverse individuals from different industries. There are a lot of self-proclaimed social media gurus out there and, while I am by far not the premier expert, I am one of the few who have managed to successfully build a large following. This book is a collection of the thoughts and experiences that helped me along the way. I hope it can be of use to you in building your network and your career.

Creating Your Profile

Like any other business endeavor, building your network requires a game plan. You will need to decide how to present yourself via your LinkedIn profile page and who you want to connect with. I cannot emphasize this enough: make sure you have an appealing and professional profile page. People will only want to connect with you if they feel there is a strategic business reason for doing so. You must have a professional profile page with correct keywords, job descriptions, industry-related terms, and most importantly, great photography. Keep in mind that a complete profile is going to be more frequently searched than an incomplete profile because it will garner more search “hits”. You need to ensure that you have your relevant work history listed on your profile and that you have up-to-date and accurate information. (If you have experiences or short-lived careers that do not impact the network you are trying to build then I would suggest simply leaving those off.)

As far as imagery is concerned, a professional profile picture is key (not a photo taken at prom or a backyard barbecue but an actual paid-for or bartered-for photo from a professional photographer.) The background photo can be a little bit more creative—use it to tell your audience about yourself. For example, I chose a photo with the caption "work harder." I think it gives a bit of insight into my personality, which is why I chose it. If you would like to take it up a notch, a graphic artist can create a professionally-designed backdrop. This could be, for example, an advertisement or marketing piece that will pique people's interest or an image that makes your page immediately recognizable. Another creative idea I have seen is the use of an emoji with a person's likeness. Others have used images of American flags and smiley faces. Depending on the nature of your position or career, I think there is a place for these types of fun, creative images. They might be a bit more tongue-in-cheek, but they do eventually accomplish the goal of making your profile stand out in a search list. Being easier to find and unique may encourage someone who may have otherwise overlooked you to take a deeper dive into your profile.

Similarly, providing logos or pictures for the company you represent in your experience list can be useful in attracting followers. Some well-known companies will already have a page on LinkedIn, in which case you can simply link to their page and their image or logo will appear on your profile page. If you own the company, you will have to manually upload these images.

Your profile and the details contained within are what **allows the LinkedIn search engine to find your profile.** Your search engine optimization (SEO) is crucial in order for the LinkedIn algorithm to pull up your profile when certain searches are made. Your LinkedIn page must therefore be optimized just like any good website. So how do you optimize yourself? It all comes down to keywords — both long tail and short tail (that is SEO speak for single-word keywords and a combination of certain keywords, respectively).

When creating your profile, think about the words and phrases people in your industry would search. You want to be descriptive while at the same time using the technical jargon and terms of art that a recruiter in your industry would use. Back in the day when I was an I.T. recruiter, I would spend hours on LinkedIn looking through profiles for specific words and key phrases. I would narrow the candidate pool using LinkedIn profiles and resumes I found on sites like Monster.com. So, if you are a Java developer, make sure that you include that in the job section of your LinkedIn profile. If you graduated magna cum laude, or you were an Eagle Scout, include it. You never know what keywords recruiters and other potential connects will use. It is better to be over-descriptive and potentially earn more views.

One trick to determine the best keywords to use is to simply type a word or phrase into the LinkedIn search and look at the auto-fill suggestions that pop up. You can use the same technique on Google search. Those auto-fill suggestions are probably the best keywords to use in your profile. The more career or business-specific you are in your profile, the more relevant you will be in searches and you will be found more often. The more often you are found, the more likely it is that someone will send you a connection request.

One trick to determine the best keywords to use is to simple type a word or phrase into the Linkedin Seatch.

Apart from the work you put into crafting your profile page yourself, one of the best things you can do is to ask people in your industry and former colleagues to write you recommendations. Recommendations build credibility and set you apart from the crowd. While I personally only have about seven or eight recommendations on my profile so far, I would suggest you go above and beyond and try to have at least a dozen endorsements on your site from different people from various walks of life all touting the benefits of working with you and your company. In addition give as many valid recommendations you can give to the highest quality individuals you can legitimately give a positive recommendation to. The reason you do this, is your recommendation is visible on that person's profile. By garnering additional traffic to your profile, people will discover you. In addition, the good will you gain will in many cases turn into huge business opportunities for you in the future. People like to do business with people they like and trust.

Networking "Old-School"

Believe it or not, one of the best methods for "growth hacking" LinkedIn is actually "going old- school": attending networking events.

> **LinkedIn Tip:**
> In the application. Inside of the "Search box" is a little QR icon. Tap on it and you can scan a LinkedIn QR code or preset your own code. Simplify, scan the code of the person standing next to you. Then you can be connected right then and do not have to worry about remember to connect later.

There are all kinds of great organizations out there whose goal is to help facilitate connections in your industry. Take advantage of these opportunities. Personally, I have found that visiting Business Network International (BNI) groups has been a great way to meet people in my market here in Minneapolis. Other great groups have been the Small Business Advisory Board here in Minnesota, Toastmasters, Network Solutions and the Chamber of Commerce. Networking can allow you to meet greatly talented people. For instance, the Think Great organization headed up by business author and Ted speaker Eric Theranger has also been invaluable opportunity to work with an amazing team of people. I was also privileged enough to connect with automation specialist Kari Switala from Wild Fig Marketing. I even had a chance to meet the founder of BNI Ivan Misner through "old school networking".

Truthfully, I have met so many remarkable people that I cannot possibly list them all here, but I am sure they know who they are and how much I appreciate their insight, expertise, and friendship.

An online resource that I have found to work very well for facilitating networking events and meetings is Meetup.com. Meetup is a hub for many different groups and for individuals seeking to connect with people with similar interests and goals. There are Cash Flow 101 (a great Robert Kiyosaki board game) clubs, book clubs, painting clubs, social media networking education organizations, business development groups, single ladies' night out events, and just about anything else you can imagine. I have found several great business development groups as well as a few digital marketing and social media marketing groups through Meetup. Utilizing this website, I am able to focus on the specific audience that I want to connect with and then, after some good old-fashioned handshakes and introductions, get to talking and networking in person.

Although meeting people in person may not be for everyone, it is typically free other than the cost of transportation, business cards, and maybe food and drinks. After meeting in person and grabbing a business card, you can e-mail your new colleague and send an invite to connect via LinkedIn. I have been collecting business cards for years. I even purchased a neat desk business card scanner that allows me to scan a business card and put it directly into a computer database. This saves me a lot of time and effort (I am not too big on data entry) and helps me maintain connections more easily. Another great tool is Evernote which allows you to take a picture of the business card and immediately sync your new contact into your Google account.

LinkedIn Tip: Once you have used Evernote and scanned in a business card. If the business card matches a LinkedIn profile then a small LinkedIn icon will show up. You tap on that, and it takes you to the persons profile and you can send an invite.

Targeting Your Audience on LinkedIn

When you are growing your network, you will have to ask yourself, "who is my audience?" If you do not know who you are targeting, then it is anyone's guess as to who will actually be in your network when you are through. Obviously, everyone's answer will be different. In my case, for example, I wanted to connect with CEO's and other high-level business owners and influencers. I needed to be a person that these important, highly talented people would want to meet. My LinkedIn profile needed to be pristine, eye-catching, and professional. You need to make sure that you portray your best self on your profile and in anything else you do online.

25 Tips for a Great LinkedIn Profile

1. Link to Your Portfolio

LinkedIn permits you to link to other websites from your profile, even in your "about" section. Take advantage of this by connecting your LinkedIn profile to your portfolio. This is especially pertinent for industries requiring extensive samples, such as graphic design or copywriting. As an added S.E.O. benefit you can choose "other" and add keywords describing the link you have added.

You may also include a link to your portfolio in the "additional information" section.

2. Carefully Consider the Personal vs. the Professional

There is no strict rule regarding where the line between the personal and the professional is drawn on LinkedIn. If your entire brand is about parenting, for example, it makes sense to include parenting tip updates from a personal perspective as long as your "CTA" (Call to Action) relates to your brand. If you are in any other field, your professional connections are probably not interested in your personal parenting experiences beyond birth and adoption announcements. Finding the appropriate space will allow you to appear friendly, personable, and engaging – while still maintaining the professionalism necessary to garner respect in your field.

3. Include Case Study Links and Statistics

For data-driven industries, you can display your ROI (Return on Investment) immediately on your profile. Add key facts and numbers, such as "increased customer retention rate by 75%", for example. Metrics surrounding revenue and productivity are particularly important, so track, focus, and display conversion and engagement rates whenever possible.

This is especially important when you are in a creative or new field, like social media management. You need to prove success in click-throughs, engagements, and conversions, not just vanity metrics such as followers.

4. Add Photos and Project Links

LinkedIn permits you to add specific projects and photos and links to that project. This allows you to go a step beyond your business profile entries and provides something visual to help capture a potential prospect or employer's attention. It is also a quick reference when you need to show an example of your work on short notice.

5. Skills and Recommendations

Skills and recommendations are two other ways to show your credibility. As long as you continue to build your network, skill endorsements will come naturally. Include a few areas of focus and people will click the button to endorse, as LinkedIn prompts them.

Recommendations are a bit trickier. Anyone can leave a recommendation for someone as long as they have worked or studied together, but it is not something most people will do without a request.

Consider asking people who:

PEOPLE ASSETS

- You still speak with regularly
- Write professionally and coherently
- Can talk about your assets in a unique way
- Has a high level of integrity and credibility

While the recommendation from a mentor that is respected, is the ultimate prize. A great resource is someone who you worked on behalf of or have worked under. This reflects well on you and helps establish you as a person of authority within your knowledge space. Other great recommendations can come from your coworkers, employees and satisfied customers.

Consider who to ask and then request a recommendation. You will have a chance to review the recommendation once it has been provided to you.

6. Your Headline

Your headline is more than your job title – it reflects your goals, especially if you are also freelancing or looking for your next big move. Instead of saying you are a “blog editor at ABC Standard”, consider something more descriptive that will allow potential employers to see you at their company, such as “Master of Content.” Another technique is to use the job title to “solve the customers problem.” As a Master of Content Guru, I help find unlimited lead sources for my clients through extraordinary story telling.

You can also use this space to highlight multiple related and unrelated fields, such as “financial advisor” and “fintech expert.”

When LinkedIn did national profile picture and free profile consultation tours in 2016, this was a significant area of focus for them. It should be for you as well.

7. Your Location

Think about your marketable location. Unless you live in a city, you may wish to consider placing yourself outside of your town. "Greater Chicago Area" is an option, for example, versus merely stating "Chicago." If you are hoping to relocate and can say as much on your LinkedIn page, indicate that in your profile to help future connections in other locations take you seriously.

Another useful tip: in today's internet world, a lot of you might be working remotely. If so, say so! A lot of companies are now looking for freelance writers, videographers, editors, web developers and more. If you have a business that allows you to work from anywhere, make sure to mention that.

8. Set Goals

Growing your popularity on LinkedIn is all about goal setting and follow through. Choose a timetable and set a realistic goal using metrics, such as page views or influencer connections. Then, check in with those goals regularly, and watch the page views, search appearances and people who viewed your profile. This is a living organism and needs TLC daily.

9. Add More Connections

After you collect business cards at an event invite those new contacts to your network. LinkedIn is your rolodex. Each time you make a new business contact (even if you do not do business together), add that contact on LinkedIn. That connection could lead to a business deal later.

Do not underestimate people new to your field, either. That college student you just added might become the next Bill Gates or Steve Jobs in ten to twenty years.

10. Write and Publish Articles

While it used to be exclusive, any LinkedIn member can now publish an article on LinkedIn. Focus on your area of expertise. This is an ideal place to provide an innovative or creative take on your industry and to show others that you think a bit differently and have something to offer.

11. Drive Traffic to Your Profile

Is your LinkedIn profile listed on your Twitter and Facebook pages? What about in your e-mail signature? Most people will not hesitate to connect with you on LinkedIn after seeing you are a member since LinkedIn is a purely professional platform, which makes connecting more straightforward.

So, do not be shy or bashful – put your LinkedIn page link in your e-mail signature and watch your connections grow.

Tip: You may also include your profile link on forums, email signatures and business cards.

12. Check Out Potential Connections

Unless he or she has the feature turned off, a potential or current connection's recent view of your profile is tracked.

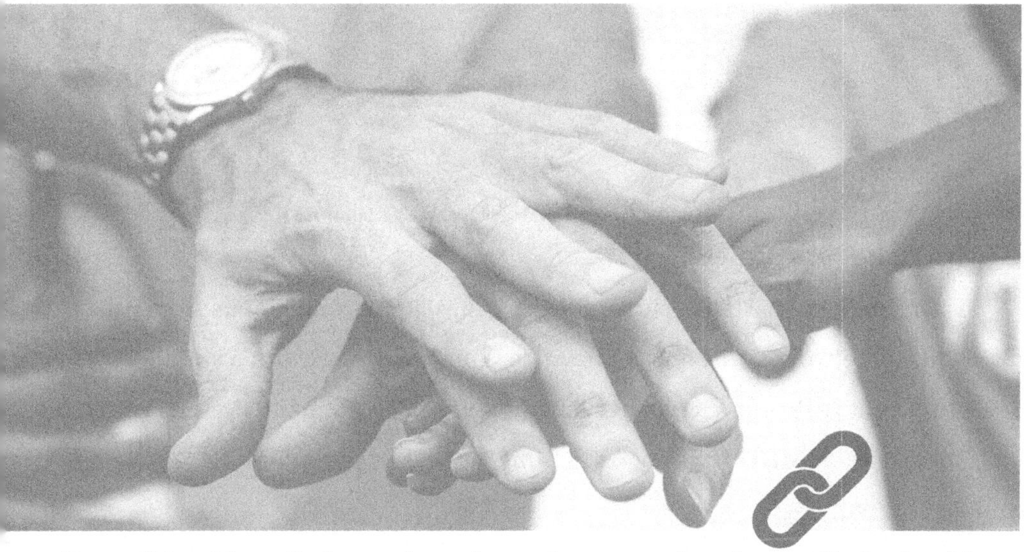

You will be able to find out where these viewers work and you will also be able to see the last several connections that viewed you. To see more, you need to upgrade to a premium account. So, make sure to take advantage of your account benefits and check your views each week.

Advanced Tip: Send a thank you note connection request to the people that view your page. Say something simple like… Thank you for visiting my profile. I hope you found something interesting. I see we have several mutual connections. I would be open to connect. (credit: Philip Calvert's tip)

13. Causes and Volunteer Experience

Volunteer work is valuable in that it shows your connection with the community as well as your values. Most people go with a safe cause such as animal or child welfare, as issues like equality and healthcare are heavily politicized.

If your causes relate to your brand or your field, definitely include them. For example, it would not seem overly political for a human rights lawyer to support Amnesty International.

However, if your causes are not related at all, do not avoid putting them on there. It is always good to show a diversity of interests.

14. Ask For Connections

Every so often, ask your personal and professional connections from other platforms to network with you on LinkedIn. You can do this with a simple Facebook or Twitter post with a link to your profile. If you use an automated social media tool like Hootesuite or MNU Dashboard, set this request to post monthly so your new connections will see it.

15. Remember: LinkedIn is a Search Engine

LinkedIn is its own search engine, which means you must optimize your profile for potential customers, J.V. partners, employers and recruiters if you wish to be found. You might want to use overly creative job titles to stand out, but few people search for something like "marketing ninja." Instead, they search for "digital marketer." You might refer to yourself instead, then, as an "innovative digital marketer."

So, even though you very well may be an "SEO Ninja", it is unlikely that people are searching for that particular skillset.

16. Google Likes LinkedIn ♥

Google and other search engines also index LinkedIn pages. If you optimize your page correctly, it should show up on a Google search, which is optimal – after all, this is what you want a potential client or employer to find when they look you up.

Use SEO (search engine optimization) copy to highlight your skills. When people search for that ability, they should find you.

Also, it goes without saying, make sure your content is correctly spelled and your grammar is on point.

17. Keep Your Profile Updated

Nothing makes you look more prepared to take on new business than an updated profile. Make sure you include the basics: company title, duties, business skills or tasks, and your tenure within the organization. In addition to updates registering with your network (in which case your connections will be notified), updated content is a positive ranking signal for Google. If you are an author, perhaps make a "job description" for each book. You can even set the dates of these books you added to coincide with when you are running a promotion as all your contacts will be told about your "anniversary date" for that book/job. This is a powerful way to get your networks attention. Remember, on LinkedIn it does not have to be your "job" it can be your "current activities". It is about who you are and your skills not the company that you are doing it for that necessarily matters.

18. Use a Professional Photo

Professional photos are essential for LinkedIn as your profile picture is the first visual impression you may get. According to LinkedIn, your face should take up 60% of the frame. They also suggest a natural smile and

making eye contact with the camera (no sunglasses?). Pick a background that is either subdued or out of focus to ensure that you are the main focus of the picture. In some instances based on your profession, throw out the basic picture and be bold, crazy and outlandish to garner the eyeballs of people looking through the postage stamp size image of the LinkedIn search. If you are someone who is a little different, embrace it and share it with the whole world.

Remember, this is not a social network like Facebook. It is best to keep it professional. Mostly..

19. Include a Background Photo

Pick a background photo that speaks to your personality or professionalism. Many LinkedIn users select something reflecting a place, hobby, or lifestyle, like a vacation spot, city, or classic car. If you are creative, consider something abstract or inspiring. This space is prime marketing space, so you may include images of you speaking or holding your new book. You can select a fun or inspiring image to use for free on sites like pixabay or unsplash – just be sure to read the image usage guidelines before snagging it. You can even get a graphic designer to help you with creating a great marketing piece.

"Is my current customer who I want to be my customer?"

Tip: I like to use something that reflects my beliefs, profession or passion.

20. Engage in Group Discussions

Being a part of a group in and of itself can facilitate connections. If you are part of a group that is more active, you can hop right in and find opportunities to learn, connect, and possibly establish yourself as an expert in your field.

One thing is for sure, engagement is never a bad thing. Even if Google does not pick up on your involvement on LinkedIn, your peers will.

21. Ask Peers for Help

Engagements – or likes, comments, and shares – dramatically increase your visibility on LinkedIn. An easy way to increase your engagements is to ask peers and followers to boost awareness of your posts and profile by liking, commenting, and sharing. Reserve this for quality content and significant announcements.

22. Get an Editor

For many positions, typos will disqualify you instantly. Vanquish the typo demon by hiring a professional editor to review your profile. If you cannot afford a professional quite yet, then use a program like Grammarly to help increase your accuracy. Just like a professional photo, this is a likely necessary investment for a LinkedIn profile of the highest quality.

23. Get a Personalized URL

LinkedIn lets you select your URL. Most people simply use their name, but you can also add your field. For example, you might write "JaneTheDigitalMarketer", International Best Selling author, or JessTiffany.

24. Stay Active on LinkedIn Messenger

LinkedIn changed its messenger program not too long ago so that it is similar to conversing on a social media network like Facebook. This takes away some of the formality of LinkedIn communication, which used to feel more like exchanging e-mails than having a real-time conversation. I personally like the change and challenge you to use it as a tool to strengthen your relationships on the platform.

Leverage LinkedIn messenger:

- Stay in touch with valuable contacts / build relationships
- Ask your contacts if you can make introductions to any connections for them
- Reach out occasionally to see if they have heard of any interesting industry changes
- Congratulate them on achievements, birthdays and business anniversaries.

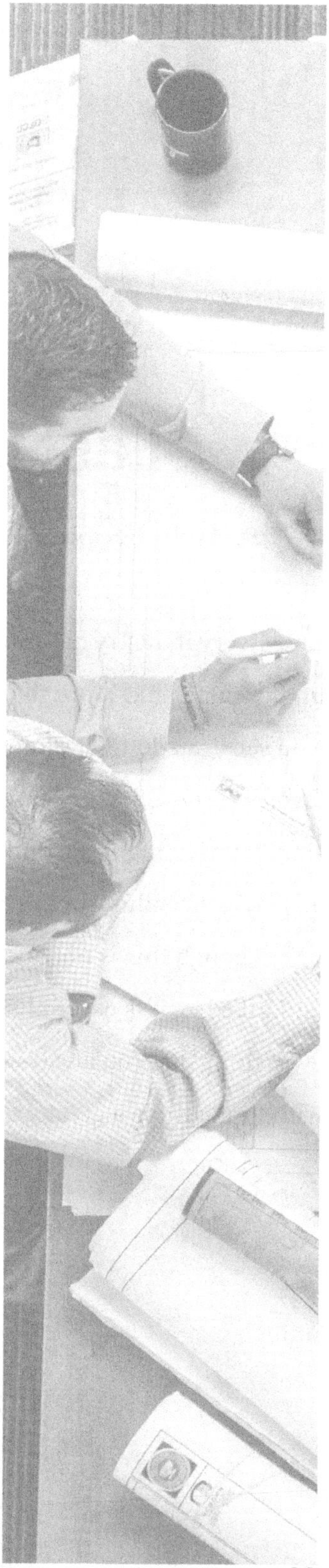

Last but not least...

25. Help People

Every industry has new people, and being helpful puts a significant deposit in the trust bank. More than that, it is not just about who you are helping – but who sees you doing it. Potential collaborators and industry influencers may look favorably on you after realizing that you help people who need it, even if that means simply providing some online resources. Plus, it is an ideal opportunity for you to display your industry expertise.

Though this is not an exhaustive list of methods to properly market yourself on LinkedIn, it is certainly a good start. Make sure to go through this list and check everything off. You always want to put your best foot forward and honing your skills with LinkedIn is a great way to do that.

Finding New Connections on LinkedIn

Deciding who you want in your network circles back to your original motivation and goals. What is it that you are going after? Who is your ideal customer? Who is your current customer? You may even have to ask yourself, "Is my current customer who I want to be my customer?" If not, now would be the best time to work on changing that.

A pitfall that many of us fall into is thinking that anybody and everybody could be or should be our customer. This approach usually dilutes the effect that we are trying to achieve by building the network in the first place. Now, if you do happen to be building a very large network, having some extraneous customers in the network is not too problematic. However, make sure you are not wasting time trying to develop something that will likely never yield results.

It goes without saying that you should be kind and courteous to your entire audience regardless of who they are, their particular belief systems, or any other distinction. I live in the Midwest of the United States, which tends be pretty homogeneous. However, as a business owner and marketer, you need to embrace diversity and inclusion and understand that there is value in various ideas and cultures. This does not mean that you have to accept all things and all behaviors but

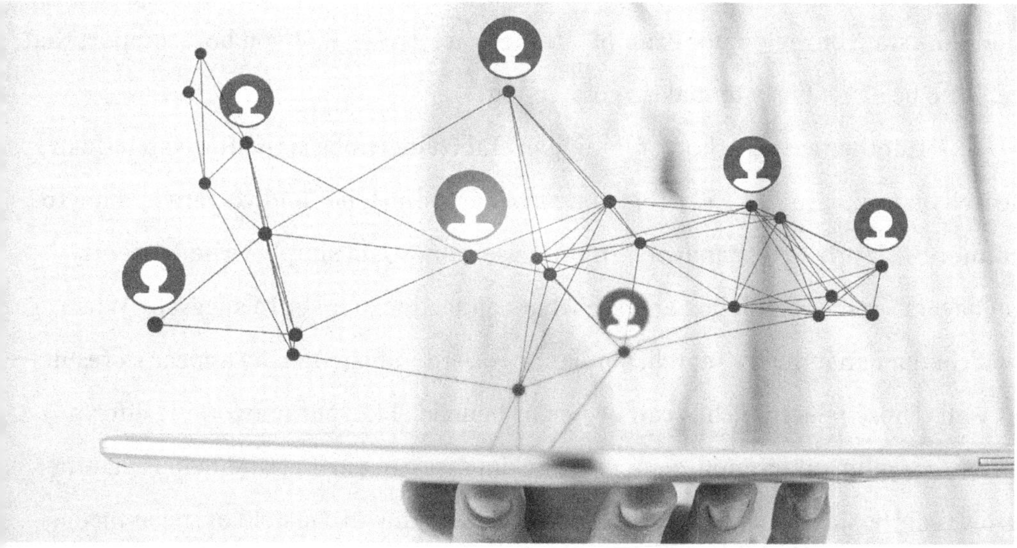

you can still respect that each and every person is unique and special in their own way and that God created them all. So, treat each and every person with the dignity and respect that they deserve. It is not your job to judge.

Once you have figured out who your audience is, you have to be able to connect with them. The most obvious method of doing so is to use LinkedIn's built-in search features. If you know the name of the person that you want to connect with, you can simply find the magnifying glass at the top of the LinkedIn webpage, type in his or her name, and hit "enter." Once the results come back you will either see multiple people with that name, if it is a common one, or perhaps just one person if it is an uncommon name. At this point, you can simply click the "connect" button or, if you want to increase your odds of connecting with that person, write a personal note and customize the invitation. If you have met the person before, you will want to remind him or her of where you met and perhaps what you talked about. When you invite somebody you have already met in person the odds are very much in your favor that the person will connect with you, hence the importance of "old-school" networking.

Another way to find the person you are looking for is to search by job title. For instance, if you are looking for a professional baseball player to market your vitamin line or chewing gum, type that job title into the search bar. When inviting people from this results list, look for indications of relatability. Perhaps you live in the same state or region, for example. If there are causes that you both support that can also be a great way to make a connection.

Another easy method of finding useful connections is to utilize an industry search on LinkedIn. Let's say that you are a carpet installer and you are looking to connect with property managers. In this case, you would simply write "property managers" in the search box and see what connections LinkedIn suggests. When you conduct an industry search, similar or related industries may appear as results as well. Those related niches can be just as beneficial in your networking efforts. Often, complimentary, non-competing businesses can partner and help each other grow their businesses. For instance, someone working in the field of social media would benefit from knowing someone who works in SEO, a graphic designer, an e-mail automation specialist, a social media content creator, or a website designer. Likewise, a plumber would do well to associate with an electrician and a handyman. In my experience, these types of connections are some of the most lucrative business relationships you can make. You can share customer lists, participate in joint ventures, barter services, and share in advertising costs. I have personally bartered for doctor visits, accounting services, SEO, social media work, and content writing. If you are a new business, these types of arrangements will be crucial to your ultimate success. I cannot emphasize enough that there really is no such a thing as a self-made person. Our success is the result of the people we associate with, the books we read, and our relationships. Thanks to connections I have made this way, time after time when I have encountered obstacles in my career I have been able to reach out to a mentor or friend for quality business advice.

Location, location, location.

Another great LinkedIn search feature is the ability to find individuals based on their location. In fact, by default, LinkedIn will search the area closest to you and find people in your local area. This is fantastic if you run a local business like a massage studio or a dental office but it is also a great point of relatability. For instance, if the chiropractor's office that you found on LinkedIn is only a mile away, you can easily say, "Hey, neighbor - my office is only a mile away. We should connect!" If you are a credit card processing company and you want to target a suburb, you can simply type in the name of that suburb. This will give you the names of hundreds – if not thousands – of individuals in your area. Keep in mind that this feature typically gives you the names of individuals, not businesses. The good thing is that you can isolate certain professions in the search as well. For example, you may want to search "chiropractor in Burnsville, Minnesota."

Building a worldwide online e-learning platform for businesses, I desire to connect with people from all over the world. The beautiful thing about LinkedIn search features and filters is that I am able to narrow down specific job titles, filter out first-degree connections so that I know I am reaching new audiences, and target specific countries. I will often use three, four, or even five filters to narrow down the exact person or type of person that I am trying to connect with. For instance, I may want to connect with a social media company that I have never contacted before that operates in Pune, India. The very next search may be for a technology Chief Information Officer from Denmark who has worked in Hong Kong. It is absolutely astounding how specific you can get. I can almost find a needle in the world's haystacks using the search features on LinkedIn.

The Power of Boolean Search:

Another search technique is called Boolean. It allows broadening or narrowing down your searches with a specific searching method that can be used with Google and many other search platforms as well.

Here are some of the basics of Boolean:

Common Techniques:

- Exact Phrase Search, place each phrase in "quotes". For example, type "Project Manager". Or "Chemical Engineering Specialist" for multi-word or muli-phrase searches. Note: LinkedIn does not support specialized quotes or symbols at this time.
- AND searches: AND searches: Type the word AND with capital letters to see results that include all of the items in your list. This typically limits your search results. For example, "Chiropractor AND therapist AND Back Doctor".
- NOT searches: Use the word NOT with capital letters immediately before a search word to exclude it from your search. This likely limits your search results. For example, "Chiropractor NOT Massage".
- OR searches: Use the word OR with capital letters to see results from a list that includes one or more search items. This usually will broaden your search results. For example, "Chiropractor OR Dentist OR Practitioner".

- Parenthetical search: To do a more advanced search, you are able to combine terms using "parentheses". For example, to find people who have "CEO" in their profiles, but exclude "assistant to CEO" or CIO, type CEO NOT (assistant CEO OR CIO).

When using Boolean in LinkedIn these are the primary allowed search keys.

1. Quotation Marks [""] or Parentheses [()]
2. AND
3. NOT
4. OR

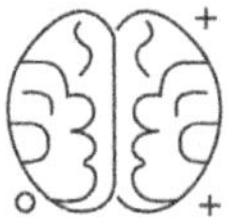

NOT ALLOWED with LinkedIn:

Things like + or -, or my favorite Boolean trick the wildcard "*" that the star means any value. So you can search your keyword and for "*.pdf" and Google brings up any file with a .pdf ending relating to the keyword entered.

One of the easiest ways to gain connections quickly is to use the "connection" section of LinkedIn to simply connect to your current e-mail contacts. This built-in utility allows you to search Outlook, Hotmail, Yahoo, Gmail, AOL and other e-mail providers' contacts lists for possible new LinkedIn connections. Once LinkedIn locates accounts that may be of interest and you authenticate the connection, you are able to send out e-mail invitations to everyone on the generated list. People who are already on LinkedIn will simply get an invitation that invites them to connect with someone that they are already connected to via email. LinkedIn will also allow you to use what is called a CSV file or a PST file to store e-mail addresses on your mobile device or an e-mail program that can be uploaded to send out invitations to connect.

You can also utilize LinkedIn's invitation by e-mail feature to invite people that you may not be able to connect with any other way. This allows you to connect with influencers, business owners, professional athletes, and others who you normally would not have the opportunity to connect with. If you can locate their e-mail addresses, you have the ability to invite them to LinkedIn to connect.

What if you do not know who exactly you want to target? You may know that you want to target a specific industry but are not sure exactly who to connect with in that industry or how. This is where a little extra creativity is needed. Typically, as an initial step, I turn to Google for answers. For example, in growing my network, I searched for New York Times best-selling business authors. I found an entire list of New York Times best-selling business books on a single blog post, copied and pasted the authors' name into LinkedIn one by one, and was able to find many of them in order to request a connection. You might also go to Amazon.com and search "business books" and find the top-selling books in the genre. Amazon also features many authors who create free e-books for promotional purposes and you can easily find their names and cross-reference those with accounts on LinkedIn.

Membership lists and contact information for organizations can also be valuable in building a network or finding potential customers and this information is often easily found online. For example, I was helping a client the other day who offers nutritional products and we were determining how to target clients in California. To our surprise, there is a California organization of chiropractors and chiropractic students and we were able to find a membership list with contact information for members. Finding this list saved us hours and hours of research and will also allow us to reach out directly through LinkedIn to make initial connections. I have also been able to locate membership rosters such as church directories online, which could prove useful to someone who owns a religious bookstore or runs a community service organization, for example. Many organizations have contact lists online with the email addresses and phone numbers published. You just have to look for them. Remember Boolean? Go into Google type in "Your target in quotes" AND "*.xls", then try "*.pdf". Many times you might find nothing and the other times you may find the perfect list for your needs.

Invitations

On LinkedIn, most of us are probably guilty of something called "spray and pray": sending a generic invite to connect versus writing a personalized message. I will admit that often times when I was trying to break into an industry or niche without any prior connections I would simply hit the "plus" button to send a generic invite. This technique is somewhat of a gamble. It can be useful for adding numbers on the off chance that the person likes your profile and decides to add you. However LinkedIn has limits of people who say they do not know you plus, it also runs the risk of garnering hate mail (in which case, on the bright side, at least you have managed to create some level of engagement, even if not the exact type you were looking for!) When this happens I typically send a message explaining that I was anxious to meet the person, apologize for not taking the time to write a personal note, and thank the person for reaching out. Hopefully, he or she accepts my apology, forgives my pathetic invitation, and finds that I might be of some service in the future. Suffice it to say, I would highly recommend personally inviting each person to connect whenever possible. Next to meeting in person, it really is your best bet for forming a meaningful connection. Remember at the end of the day it is about the relationship anyway. Quantity with quality is the aim.

I could probably write an entire book on the art of crafting the perfect invitation but, in a nutshell, you will want to welcome the person and tell him or her about yourself. You will want to talk about his or her occupation and try to find some common ground. For example, when I am talking to someone in the landscaping industry I like to share a story about a great friend I had growing up who was a landscaper. I like to talk about how hard he worked, the long hours he put in, and the sweat, the blood, and the body aches I know he put into his work. I say that I know how hard the work is and how dedicated and diligent you must be to be a

professional landscaper. Why do I do this? A few reasons. First, I really do believe landscapers work incredibly hard. Second, I want the landscaper to understand that I can relate to the daily struggle to run a landscaping business. Third, by relating I build a rapport that encourages the beginning of good communication and possibly a friendship. A personal invitation allows this to happen; "spray and pray" does not. People like to connect with people who are friendly and trustworthy. Your job as a networker is to be a relationship-builder. This is done by creating rapport and offering reciprocity. You do not have to find common ground solely on the basis of work and career. You can also talk about family, hobbies, or passions that people have listed on their profile, affiliations or organizations they give time to, groups they are involved with, favorite sports teams, and past employers. Gleaning information from their profile will help you find ways you can relate to one another and build a relationship.

The key to making personal invites for these potential connections is to let them know who you are, why you are connecting with them, and what you hope to accomplish. This will make them more likely to accept your invitation. This does not have to be a long, wordy message. It can be as simple as highlighting a common interest, common group, or mutual connection. I have gained many connections simply by saying:

"Hey John, I see we have 35 mutual acquaintances so I figured I should probably know you too. I suppose I probably met you one time and don't even remember it. I'm terrible with names! Love to be connected, let me know if I can be of service. Cheers – Jess."

I might also invite someone who has a similar job title saying something along the lines of:

"Stan, I see you're a CEO here the Minneapolis area. I am surprised we have not met at a networking event yet. I do like to connect with other local CEO's in case our paths cross and we may be able to do some business together in the future. Would be great to connect with you proactively. Let me know how I can help you. I do know a lot of great people if you need an introduction. Love to serve – Jess."

As a carpet installer, you may send an invite to a property manager you have found through an industry search saying something like:

Hello David, I see you are in the property management industry and I serve people in your industry by installing quality carpet. I think I could be a valuable resource for you in the future if something bad happens and you need a quick turnaround for carpets. Love to connect, just in case. - Mr. Carpet

Connecting with Influencers

One of the hottest topics these days is the rise of social media "influencers." How do you get a hold of one? How do you become one? Well, for starters, Google it. I was able to find an article discussing the top 100 influencers on social media. Most people would simply decide it was interesting reading and move on. What I did was try to locate these influencers on LinkedIn and connect. Luckily, the article I read

included clickable Twitter handles so I was able to simply click, connect, and follow who I could. Do not be afraid to cross platforms. One of the most popular influencers I connected with accepted my invitation because I had mentioned I was already a Twitter follower. (I should note that I had engaged him on Twitter many times before I invited him to connect on LinkedIn. Building rapport and trust involves communication, and because I had communicated with this person many times he probably felt more comfortable connecting on LinkedIn.)

Often influencers are not easily accessible or searchable on LinkedIn or Google. Many times you will have to do some digging. Other great resources are the Better Business Bureau, the Secretary of State website, or Hoover's. Once you have done your homework and found the person's contact information, the person will be more likely to connect with you because he or she will know that either you know someone or you went through a whole lot of trouble to connect.

You can become an influencer overtime yourself by connecting with enough other influencers. However, in order to do that, keep in mind that you must have a profile that demonstrates that you are a person that they would want to connect with in the first place.

Become and influencer by connecting with other influencers.

A Brief History of Growth Hacking

The internet has not only changed the way entrepreneurs and businesses market to the world, it has also brought us new techniques and tools. One of the most interesting developments has been the birth of "growth hacking", a technique that took root around 2010 and has exploded since then. The term was coined by Sean Ellis, founder and CEO of Qualaroo. (Yes, I was able to network with Mr. Ellis on Twitter and LinkedIn. We're not best buddies or anything, but give me time - I grow on people like a mold or fungus.)

What is Growth Hacking?

Understanding what growth hacking is all about starts with learning about its history and how it has been used and exploited. Growth hacking is a form of marketing based on the premise that there is limited startup capital available for growing a business. However, growth hacking techniques can be used by entrepreneurs small and large. Growth hacking focuses on the product's growth potential and on being innovative, scalable, and connecting to the potential user. Unlike traditional marketing methods that separate the design and effectiveness of the product from the overall marketing effort, growth hacking utilizes these factors to maximize the product's full potential. This is essentially guerilla marketing in terms of the capital used for promotion. Growth hacking focuses on growing the business as rapidly as possible. The underlying principle is that a company that is growing can overcome many of the challenges it will face as it expands. Only when the level of growth has reached a pre-set point do other forms of marketing come into play.

Growth hacking redefines the term "product" itself. In the past, "product" meant a physical item such as a shampoo, car, or air conditioner. With the rise of the internet, companies like Facebook or Twitter are considered products. This means that intellectual materials, software programs, and the like are now considered products to be promoted just like their physical counterparts.

Origins

In 2010 Sean Ellis coined the term "growth hacker", which he defined as someone whose true commitment is growth and who directs all resources to improving growth potential. The concept was expanded upon by Andrew Chen, who wrote an article entitled, "Growth Hacker is the new VP Marketing." In a 2012 publication in TechCrunch, Aaron Ginn noted that a growth hacker is someone whose mindset revolves around data, creativity, and curiosity. My definition of growth hacking is much simpler: for me, growth hacking is doing things to grow your business rapidly without much money.

In 2013, Ellis joined Dylan La Com, Everette Taylor, Morgan Brown, and several others to start "GrowthHackers", a community that offered software as a service (SaaS) which augmented the growth process. That same year, the Second Annual GrowthHackers Conference in San Francisco featured individuals who had used the techniques on social media sites such as Twitter, YouTube, and LinkedIn. Ellis' success at setting up several internet companies and helping them to achieve remarkable growth in a short period of time quickly earned him a powerful reputation. After the companies he assisted were able to hold Initial Public Offerings, Ellis became one of the most powerful figures in internet marketing. His basic technique was to come in, set up the right systems, change mindsets to a growth mentality, and then leave so that he could help others. Today, growth hacking has developed to the point where it has become a mainstream tactic of modern marketing.

Growth hacking is not just another form of marketing: it requires a different skill set. Ellis discovered this quickly when he tried to find a replacement. Those educated in traditional marketing were not well-suited to the job of growth hacking. So, unsurprisingly, Ellis began looking for growth hackers instead of traditional marketers—for people who believed that growth was the only goal considered worthwhile.

From Dropbox, to Hotmail, to AirBnB, and Beyond

Because growth hacking views delivery systems like social media as products, you can use products to boost the sales of other products. This redefines the meaning of "growth" in today's internet world. An early example was YouTube adding a "confirm channel subscription" link to the end of its URL. It managed to grow

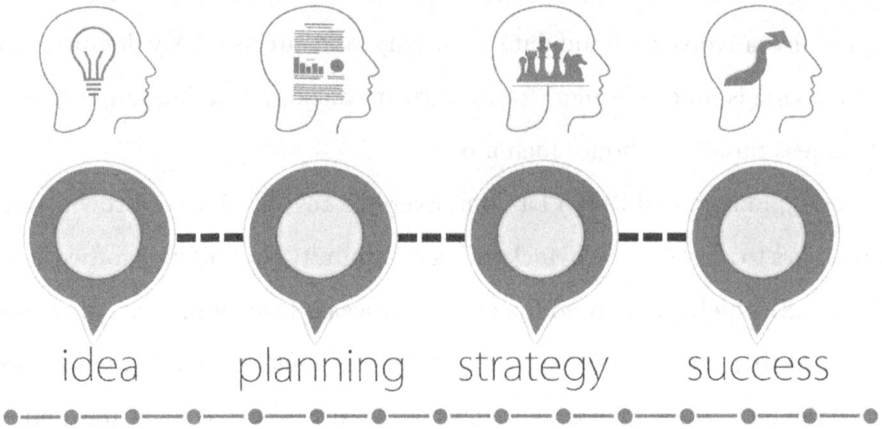

its subscription base by 400%. Another brilliant YouTube hack was the "embed" feature. Viewers could share a video on their blog or website and all links led back to YouTube, building credibility and logo recognition on millions of sites across the Internet.

Another example is Dropbox, which provides you with free cloud storage if you can get someone to sign up with you. Sean Ellis managed to take Dropbox and grow it tremendously using basic concepts of growth hacking.

AirBnB has managed to take it a step further by bringing together technology and clever thinking. AirBnB hijacked Craigslist property listings and brought in its base of support through automated listing generators. Called "post to Craigslist", it was a remarkably simple – but powerful – idea that helped its clients access a powerful website to aid in scaling the business when they did not have the needed inventory.

Twitter uses growth hacking and data to grow its user base by getting a user to follow five to ten people as soon as they start. Simple e-mail sites like Hotmail can also be used as products to promote and sell other products, creating a chain that boosts the company's overall growth. When Hotmail began its "P.S. I Love You" campaign, providing a link to invite others to the site, it was an example of growth hacking at its finest. Hotmail grew massively because of this "hack" to over 12 million e-mail accounts and, of course, Microsoft then paid $400 million to purchase Hotmail.

LinkedIn went from 2,000,000 to 200,000,000 users by creating public profiles that anyone could search. People knew if they wanted to be found online, they needed to be on LinkedIn. LinkedIn then took it a step further by importing members' e-mail contacts and sending those contacts an invite to connect through LinkedIn. This had a viral effect, spreading LinkedIn across the world.

There are many examples of growth hacking today that account for the massive rise of small businesses, entrepreneurs, and even large corporations. Sean Ellis' vision has resulted in a distinct change in how businesses grow and overcome many of the challenges faced in the start-up phase. His simple but powerful approach continues to expand.

It is important for business owners to remember that growth hacking does not just focus on a single product, but on using different products and pushing them to their maximum potential. Getting the most out of growth hacking results in creating large businesses from small ones through clever use of the internet and stacking products with delivery systems with other products.

Growth hacking has been an essential component in growing my business because a large percentage of the money I had was tied into my regular, traditional business. When starting my current venture, with the Marketing and Networking University, I did not have the luxury of a large budget. So I had to scrape, plunder, work hard, and growth-hack my way to some level of success. I may not have had an eloquent definition of growth hacking or a blueprint, but I started to use growth hacking techniques I learned or figured out for myself along the way to move my business forward. The same techniques – or, at least, the same ideas behind the techniques – are universal and can be used by individuals to grow their social media presence just like a company would use them to grow across the Internet. I will proudly admit that I am a "hack of growth hackers." The really good growth hackers tend to utilize a lot more data more efficiently and are good with numbers, graphs, figures, and statistics. However, what I lack in data and statistics I make up for with creativity, trial and error, persistence, and working my tail off. Using growth hacking principles growing LinkedIn is more about sourcing information, gathering e-mail addresses and leveraging what you have available. By being creative and using available resources you can significantly grow your network, without delving into the world of data analytics too much. However, it is fair to say if you do use data to back up what you are doing, you will likely have more success even faster.

Growth Hacking Tools

One growth hacking tool that is regularly used by many is a chrome extension called **"E-mail Hunter."** E-mail Hunter will search a company's webpage for e-mail addresses that contain the company name or address. This would be used when your target person requires you know their email address to send a connection. Obviously getting referred to these people is a preferred method. However, there are times when you feel the connection is valuable to your network, or there is not enough time to do the preferred method of connecting. So, if I were to go to the Google.com chrome extension for E-mail Hunter, I would get a list of ten e-mail addresses related to that company. (E-mail Hunter has a free version that provides up to ten free e-mail addresses.) I have used E-mail Hunter to find connections at venture capital companies and to scrape news organization websites for the e-mail addresses of reporters. I can even go to the websites of famous public speakers like Anthony Robbins and find e-mail addresses for people within their organizations. I have also searched startup companies in related niches, gathered e-mail addresses, and contacted those people to connect on LinkedIn.

You can also use E-mail Hunter to search LinkedIn profiles for valid e-mail addresses. If E-mail Hunter is unable to locate a valid e-mail address for an individual, it takes the person's namc and company name and uses the company's standard e-mail address format to formulate a likely e-mail address for the person you are trying to contact. *(Update e-mail hunter struck a deal with LinkedIn and no longer works on LinkedIn but still works great everywhere else. (New competitors have swooped in to offer this service like Sales Lift Prospector and Lead Leaper.)

A similar program is **"E-mail Stripper."** This program basically scours the web for e-mail addresses related to certain keywords, like a company name. Now, E-mail Stripper has some drawbacks. Often, I have gotten results that were likely either fake e-mail addresses or computer-generated e-mail addresses used within a company for specific tasks – something like YZK6RT.573zzzzzyyy234$ – p@ yahoo.com or some other strange variant. However, on the plus side, many results are valid for the search term. A good data person could create databases with all of the e-mail addresses and then track which ones were valid so that he or she could reach out to connect on LinkedIn.

Another great growth hack is utilizing freelancers and outsourced services to help gather information. There are many resources available today: Elance.com, Freelancer, Upwork, and even Amazon have become involved in the freelance industry. The site I use most frequently is Upwork. The main reason I chose Upwork is that it has been around for a while. I have found the platform very easy to use and I am able to find an adequate number of contractors for whatever task I need completed. Another great platform for quick and easy jobs is Fiverr.com. Essentially, as its name suggests, any small task you want done is completed for just five dollars. Over the last couple of years, however, the site has been changing to allow for more expensive tasks or packages so it is becoming harder to find things that are just five dollars anymore. That said, there are still a ton of things you can get done relatively inexpensively. You can have contractors share a Twitter post with a bunch of people or design a very simple logo for your group page on Facebook. The old adage "you get what you pay for" is certainly something to keep in mind. However, sometimes you do find contractors that are absolute gems and you keep giving them work over and over again because they do good work and they do it inexpensively.

The main task that I had outsourced during my networking operation was the gathering of contact information for specific people. I mentioned earlier that almost any group you want to find is searchable on the internet and that many sites include e-mail addresses, names, phone numbers, and addresses for their members. If you were targeting churches to offer choir robe pressing services, for example, you might Google the name of the church organization that you were interested in. You would likely find the name of a primary church and then a list of satellite churches, their phone numbers, and the pastors' e-mail addresses. The real estate industry is also especially easy to search as each agent has his or her own unique phone number, e-mail address, and a particular office and location. You could harvest agents' e-mail addresses and other data online and compile an Excel sheet with the data. You could then isolate the column containing contact information, place that information into a Word file, format the file properly for LinkedIn, and send invitations to all of your prospective real estate connections on LinkedIn at once. The downfall of this method, unfortunately, is that you do not get the opportunity to personalize each message. However, you can add a lot of people very rapidly, assuming they accept

your invitation. Again, this is greatly dependent on the quality of your profile.

(You must use caution here as LinkedIn tracks how many people say they do not know you and can block you from adding additional people.)

If you are willing to spend some money you can buy targeted lists, but this carries some risks. First, the lists that are sold are not exclusive and therefore the same people are potentially targeted multiple times. Some lists and directory sites also tend to be incomplete or inaccurate. You might also choose to pay to gain access to an organization's member list. For example, if you were a mowing company looking to partner with some landscapers you could join a landscaping association in order to gain access to its membership list. Depending on the cost of the membership, it might very well be worth the investment in order to gain access to prospective leads for your business.

After I had already reached 10,000 connections, I discovered a useful, versatile chrome extension called "Linked Helper." As previously mentioned always be cautious when using these types of automated plug-ins because LinkedIn can potentially block your account if it deems such a plug-in is in violation of the terms of service. The program itself places certain limitations on you for that exact reason. So, I have tested it somewhat sparingly. I have used it quite successfully, however, to invite second-degree connections (people you are not connected with directly but who are connected to one or more people in your network) and even third-degree connections (who neither you nor your anyone in your network is connected to). How this application seems to get past any scrutiny is that it literally uses LinkedIn the same way you do. You can watch on the screen as it clicks on individual buttons and types out your message letter by letter.

Basically, to use Linked Helper, you create a search with the exact keywords you are looking for in a prospective connection. You can use filter or even Boolean search results. Then in Linked Helper click "collect" and the program collects each potential contact until you click "stop collecting." You have the opportunity to name and save the list for later. Once you are done collecting possible connections, you can create a custom message, which, again, you will absolutely want to do. One important thing to note: if you have too many invites out or too many people say they do not know you after receiving an invite, you can be forced to provide an e-mail address for every person you want to connect with going forward. So, you want to make your messages as compelling as possible so this does not happen. After you have created your custom message, you can adjust how many invitations to send out for the day. The maximum number Linked Helper will send in one day is 80. I would recommend sticking to closer to 20-30 a day.

I have been on the "naughty list" for a period of time prior to when Linked Helper was around for sending to many invites early in my connection building days. This was when I did the "spray and pray" method earlier on. When you are on the list they start to ask you how you know someone or require the email for every connection. This really slows down the connection process. So trust me do not overuse a tool like this. Even without a tool you can overdo it. At the time when I was prompted for more information in order to connect, you could just go on your mobile and connect to the same person and it would not prompt for email or more information. Plus, of course I could find most people's email addresses. So it did not stop me growing my connections but it did slow down the process. It also was very annoying that you had to jump through hoops when you want to connect with your friend from high school. They would connect 100% of the time but of course you don't have their email handy. Again, be careful not to get overzealous. You can grow fast without penalty if you have an attractive profile that appeals to your targeted audience, personalize invitations, and show sincerity. Do these things and you will likely not make the "naughty list".

USE CAUTION
LI tracks how many people say they do not know you and black you from adding additional people

Getting back to Linked Helper, it will also open the profile of each person on your list and endorse him or her for certain skills. By default, the program will endorse three skills. However, you can choose as many as you like. Many people will endorse you back as a courtesy or send you a "thank you", which opens up an opportunity for conversation, which ultimately is the goal.

Linked Helper will also browse through profile pages on "auto visitor" to give the appearance of your interest in people's profiles. This, again, can lead to conversation and connection requests. People appreciate when others show interest in them. It might seem insincere at first thought but, keep in mind, showing interest can lead to conversation, meaningful relationships, and possible collaboration.

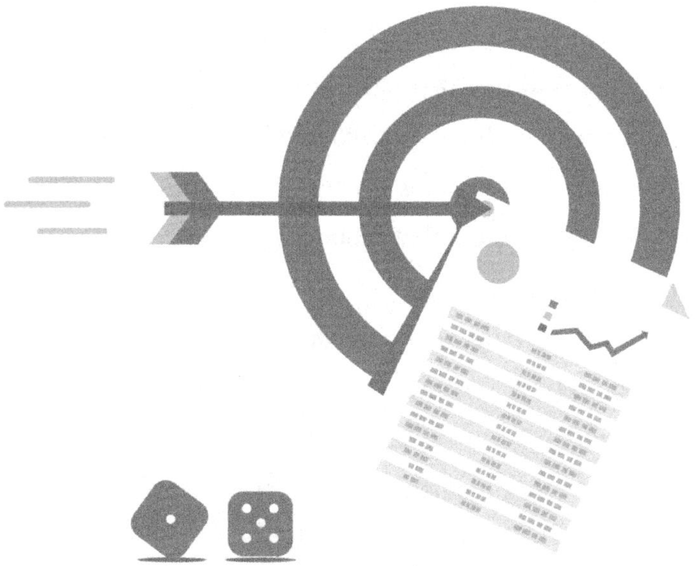

Linked Helper also allows you to cancel invites, which is useful because if you send out too many invites LinkedIn will prevent you from sending any more. Alternatively, you can go to the "pending invitations" section of your LinkedIn account and click "withdraw" hundreds or thousands of times. If you are a seasoned growth hacker, you can simply utilize a script. When logged in to LinkedIn on the Windows platform, right-click on the screen and click "inspect" to see the backend code of the page you are on. Toward the bottom of the code area, you will see the word "command" and below that there will be an empty line where you can paste script. The script I found withdraws approximately 50 invitations at a time so, if we run it 10 to 15 times, all of our pending invites will be withdrawn. The following is the script I used, but keep in mind that if LinkedIn makes any changes to its website the script may no longer be valid:

```
var i = 1;                    // set your counter to 1
function myLoop () {          // create a loop function
  setTimeout(function () {
    i++;                      // increment the counter
    if (i < 50) {             // if the counter < 10, call the loop function
      myLoop();               // .. again which will trigger another
      $('.button-tertiary-medium-muted').click();
      console.log(i);
    }                         // .. setTimeout()
  }, 4000)
}
myLoop();
```

Technology is constantly changing and I have seen quite a few chrome extensions and similar programs come and go fairly rapidly, but it is still worthwhile to keep on top of new programs and use your time more effectively wherever possible.

Linked Helper also has an export feature that you can use to make lists of your connections. This can also be accomplished through LinkedIn itself by requesting exports of all your connections. A great "lead generation" feature is also included. This is the ability to automatically send messages to your connections. The reason I say this is a "lead generation" feature versus just a "communication system" is that it can compose lists by profession, title, or any other parameter. I can send out a single message to a specific targeted niche, and quickly. I can then easily isolate and categorize those who are interested in what I am communicating about and those who are not. It is reminiscent of "cold" e-mail and phone call techniques except that these connections are already "warm" which will lead to a higher return on investment. Up until I reached 10,000 connections, I had to work a lot harder to make good connections. Now, I can simply push a button to target the correct audience, utilize the correct message or invitation, and then focus my efforts on building the relationships with the time I have left over.

Technology is constantly changing and I have seen quite a few chrome extensions and similar programs come and go fairly rapidly, but it is still worthwile to keep on top of new programs and use your time more effectively wherever possible

Using Growth Hacking Techniques to Attract Invitations

Up until now we have focused on how you can make connections yourself. Let's now look at a few ways you can try to use growth hacking techniques to get requests coming your way. One of the easiest ways to get other people to connect with you is to simply surf profiles on LinkedIn. Many premier LinkedIn subscribers have an option to see who has visited their profile. Some of these people will turn around and send you a connection request out of curiosity. So, find people in your niche, visit their sites, read their profiles, and click on their shared links. I have found that if you go to the same person's page a few times within a week the likelihood of receiving a connection request from that percent increases significantly.

Another somewhat obvious method is, again, to make sure that you have the correct keywords on your profile page. If you are in a person's target market or you have similar interests, he or she may decide to connect with you.

Joining the right groups can also make a significant difference in being found. People like to connect with individuals with similar interests. So, do some research and find out what groups your target audiences join and join those same groups. Do your best to be active in these groups, sharing and commenting on content to increase your visibility. Every time you comment, your name and picture shows up. More visibility = more connections over time. By engaging your target audience in individual conversations in the comments and "tagging" people, you can start a conversation and hopefully a relationship. A very easy way to attract some connections to you is find an article that a mentor has posted that has a fair amount of traction. Go through and like multiple comments, add comments to others comments and tag people that may have a shared interest in these topics. This will draw in your mentors followers to connect to you, and your dream mentor may see you engaging with his followers and it can cause curiosity to know who you are.

Conclusion

At the end of the day success on the platform gets down to relationship building. It is crucial that we continue to build great relationships and strengthen your inner circle of people. Simultaneously, we grow a large passive network of our ideal customers, future employees, dream mentors and people that you can relate too. Overtime these people will see your name, your company, your products and other things you share. You are literally building your future sales funnel today. It is great to pay for advertising through Facebook and Google, and it is likely faster. However, for essentially free, you can build trust with your perfect dream list of business people that you strategically selected. I encourage you to build your LinkedIn following with a purpose. Take some of the tips and growth hacks in the book and implement them. Make sure you consider terms of service for the platform provider as you do not want to build your network only to end up blocked. If you build a great looking profile that is optimized for search, you will by default gain more traction on LinkedIn. Add strategic inviting to your regimen, Reach out to past customers and school mates to have some early wins. Begin to introduce your connections to others, and reciprocity will kick in. Also do not forget to ask to be introduced to the ideal clients they are connected to. You have the ability to build an amazing funnel for your business! Now can be your time. As Zig Ziglar used to say,

"See you at the top!"

Contact Information:

Jess Tiffany
jess@mnudigital.com
612.440.8286
www.mnudigital.com

About the Author
Kudos
Reviews

About the Author

Jess Tiffany, born in the little town of Ellendale, North Dakota moved to the sprawling metropolis of Minot, ND with a massive 30,000 other folks. Grew up loving sports like tennis, basketball, baseball and any other sport he could play including kick boxing and martial arts later in his early twenties. Jess has always been entrepreneurial and a sales guy. He of course did the lemonade stands and such as a younger guy. Then when he was 12 he talked the Pastors wife into letting him earn a commission selling her Avon products. Little church ladies couldn't resist his smile and his simple plea to buy some products from him. Later he sold cars, did cold calling telemarketing, multil-level marketing, fast food and then ending up working with computers for several years. During this time he also had started his own business selling various products and services while working his I.T. job.

Next he followed a red head to Minneapolis where she had been living and married her. Jess took a high paying corporate I.T. gig while still running his online products company. Soon after marriage came the first kid and Jess committed to work hard for his family. He later had several corporate jobs including one he really enjoyed running many of the training courses across 3M campus. This job is what ultimately gave him a passion to combine education with his business and sales ventures.

Marketing and Networking University

Jess Tiffany is the C.E.O. of the Marketing and Networking University which is an online business education marketplace. There are all kinds of e-learning companies out there and they only can get a person so far. We aim to bridge the gap from education to execution. Knowledge without application is essentially worthless. We are convinced by providing the right resources, tools, education, and support more businesses can reach the million-dollar mark and beyond. Come and enroll or teach your business skills at the Marketing and Networking University today and let's build your business.

Kudos For Jess

Jess has been quoted in the Huffington Post, Monster.com, eContent, Star Tribune, Docurated, Activerain, Marketersmedia, CEOBlogNation, Klaviyo, Antavo, Salestools.io, Philadelphia Daily News, and many many more. Contributor to Six-Figure Coach Magazine, The Huffington Post (Former) and Authority Magazine. Included in Who's Who in America and the World. Listed as a Top 250 Growth

REVIEWS

Graham Riley, Social Business Strategies LLC

"Growth Hacking: LinkedIn Strategies", the new book by Jess Tiffany presents an easy-to-follow, practical, achievable and concise guide that (if followed) can make all the difference to elevating and enhancing your LinkedIn presence. The book is full of practical ideas and techniques with insights that can be utilized by the complete novice or LinkedIn super-user."

Graham Riley is a social media expert on various platforms, his competencies comprise of lead generation, employer branding services, creation of websites, mapping the customer journey and digital transformation consulting. As the Managing Director of Social Business Strategies LLC, Graham combines his operational leadership, social media and lead generation skills to bring about radical growth for clients.

LinkedIn: https://www.linkedin.com/ingrahamkeithriley/
Website: http://www.sbspartnersllc.com

Shaun Rein, Founder and Managing Director of the China Maket Research Group

LinkedIn is one of the most powerful tools for improving sales and building brands; yet, most executives do not know how to craft the right profile, build a following, or interact with their audience in a way that generates leads and helps close deals. Tiffany's book masterfully walks executives through the ins and outs on how best to set increase brand awareness and profits.

Shaun Rein is the Founder and Managing Director of the China Market Research Group (CMR), the world's leading strategic market intelligence firm focused on China. He works with boards, CEOs and senior executives of Fortune 500 and leading Chinese companies, private equity firms, SMEs and long/ hedge funds to develop their China growth and investment strategies.

LinkedIn: https://www.linkedin.com/in/shaunrein/
Website: http://www.cmrconsulting.com.cn/
• Buy Shaun's Latest book: The War for China's Wallet: Profiting from the New World Order

Karen Amundson, Diamond Hawk Unlimited, LLC

A must read for anyone serious about effectively growing their business. LinkedIn is such a reputable platform and the majority of us don't use it at all or don't use it correctly. Mr. Tiffany's

no non-sense approach, advice and expert tips will launch your business to the next level. By strategically building an amazing network, you will not only be able to connect to your dream clients, you will be influencing their connections as well."

Karen L Amundson took her love of the outdoors and her 20+ years of outdoor adventure travel experiences to create Diamond Hawk Unlimited, LLC. She is the go-to expert for team building adventures and customized travel planning.

Karen ignites everyone around her with her unique blend of corporate training, know-how as an entrepreneur, and a lifetime of backcountry wilderness and scuba diving travel experience. Audiences are drawn in by her fun, animated style as she shares her compelling stories and insights for success. Prepare to feel energized and inspired!

LinkedIn: https://www.linkedin.com/in/karenlamundson/
Website: http://www.diamondhawkunlimited.com/

Rebecca Rausch, Neon Lizard Creative | Brand Strategy/Print/Social Media

As a professed self-help junkie, trying to hone my craft and grow my business at every given opportunity, Jess Tiffany's book, "Growth Hack[in]G Secrets "is a gem. Current and on point, this is a fairly quick read, chock full of concise tips and tricks that are each game changers. Serious leaders, this book is for you.

Neon Lizard Creative is a design and marketing specialty firm. For over 20+ years, Neon Lizard Creative has created award-winning print/digital messaging & brand design. From start ups to Fortune 500, NLC can help your company make a memorable impact in a saturated market. Follow NLC on LinkedIn or visit their site to receive mindful marketing wisdom and see the latest design victories.

LinkedIn: https://www.linkedin.com/in/rebeccarauschnlc/
Website: https://www.neonlizardcreative.com/

Sam Hurley, Internet Phenom

Jess has covered the very fundamentals of LinkedIn in this book — Many that even marketers fail to utilize or grasp in the first place. If you're looking to efficiently & effectively grow a targeted network on this incredible social platform, get your teeth stuck right in! The bonus? Jess has successfully built his own engaged LinkedIn following, so what you read is drawn from real experience.

Sam Hurley is the Guy Who Went From 'Nobody' to #1 Marketing Influencer in 15 Months (Without a Website). Sam has become an internet phenomenon with his unprecedented speed of growth via social media. He has been featured in vast number of business and marketing periodical in the world. Sam Hurley is a lateral-thinking, people-focused digital marketer — holding solid experience in both agency and client-side settings. He now runs his own global personal branding and influencer marketing business: OPTIM-EYEZ. Catch Sam on Twitter and LinkedIn for cosmic amounts of helpful material on entrepreneurship and marketing!

LinkedIn: https://www.linkedin.com/in/hurleysam/
Website: https://www.optim-eyez.co.uk/

Joanne Weiland, Founder & Chief Collaborations Officer LinktoEXPERT

You can spend the next couple years uncovering the secrets of growth hacking or you can read Jess Tiffany's summary in his insightful well written, easy to understand book: GROWTH HACK[in]G Secrets. We are honored that Jess Tiffany is a member of our Collaborative Cloud Community: www.JessTiffany.LinktoEXPERT.com Jess was the first person to tell me we are growth hackers, I didn't understand what that meant at that time, but now I am proud to be a growth hacker!

In 2007 Joanne Weiland invented LinktoEXPERT, to implement your ideas with ease by collaborating and leveraging each other's education, experience & expertise which ultimately results in extraordinary success.

LinkedIn: https://www.linkedin.com/in/jweiland/
Website: http://www.linktoexpert.com

David Brier, Branding & Rebranding Unleashed I Speaker I Author: Bestselling Book "BRAND INTERVENTION" responsible for $1B in sales

Jess outlines—like a GPS on a roadmap—how to max out LinkedIn, which can be a rough road if you don't know the terrain that's peculiar to LinkedIn. Knowing this terrain is like having a 'treasure map' that gets you to where to find the hidden treasure without being eaten alive, or hitting dead ends.

A Fast Company expert blogger and the subject of numerous articles in Forbes, ADWEEK, Huffington Post and Business Insider, David Brier is the recipient of the Presidential Ambassador for Global Entrepreneurship medallion, presented to David by Shark Tank star and NY Times bestseller Daymond John.

LinkedIn: https://www.linkedin.com/in/davidbrier/
Website: https://www.risingabovethenoise.com

Dr. Michael Hennes, Owner/Clinical Director Limitless Health MNs

Jess Literally wrote the book on growing your professional network. Like all good things, you have to put in the work but with Jess' help, I managed to grow my network 30% in just under a month.

Dr. Michael finds great joy and satisfaction from giving hope to people who continue to seach for answers to their chronic health problems. The secret to his success is found in his comprehensive and cutting-edge approach. His 5-Dimensional Matrix combines the latest breakthroughs in Brain Science, Nutrition, and Physical Medicine into a plan unique to you.

LinkedIn: https://www.linkedin.com/in/dr-michael-hennes-91b7bb63/
Website: https://www.limitlesshealthmn.com

Jeffrey Hayzlett, Primetime TV & Podcast Host, Speaker, Author and Part-Time Cowboy

One of the cornerstones of success is surrounding yourself with the right peple. It's not just quantity, but quality, too. Jess' book focuses on the strategies needed to make meaningful long-lasting connections to make your circle bigger. It's all about who you know!

Jeffrey Hayzlett is a change agent, focusing on leadership, innovation and change management to drive business growth. His signature humor and big, bold approach engages audiences to start thinking differently about their business. Hayzlett motivates audiences to become change agents and leaves them inspired to overcome difficult situations and lead with strength and courage. With decades of experience in business growth, communications, leadership and marketing, Hayzlett shares his many successes – and failures – to give your company a new perspective on creativity, innovation, marketing, management and customer service.

LinkedIn: https://www.linkedin.com/in/hayzlett/
Website: http://hayzlett.com